Color the Names of God

Artwork by Marie Michaels

HARVEST HOUSE PUBLISHERS
EUGENE, OREGON

Scripture quotations are from the:

New American Standard Bible®, © 1960, 1962, 1963, 1968, 1971, 1972, 1973, 1975, 1977, 1995 by The Lockman Foundation. Used by permission. (www.Lockman.org)

New King James Version®. Copyright © 1982 by Thomas Nelson, Inc. Used by permission. All rights reserved.

Holy Bible, New International Version®, NIV®. Copyright © 1973, 1978, 1984, 2011 by Biblica, Inc.® Used by permission. All rights reserved worldwide.

The Holy Bible, New Living Translation, copyright ©1996, 2004, 2007, 2013 by Tyndale House Foundation. Used by permission of Tyndale House Publishers, Inc., Carol Stream, Illinois 60188. All rights reserved.

Design and production by Harvest House Publishers, Inc.

COLOR THE NAMES OF GOD

Copyright © 2016 by Dugan Design Group
Published by Harvest House Publishers
Eugene, Oregon 97402
www.harvesthousepublishers.com

ISBN 978-0-7369-6853-9 (pbk.)

Printed in United States of America

16 17 18 19 20 21 22 23 / VP-JC / 10 9 8 7 6 5 4 3

A Good Place to Begin

This coloring book is for artists of all ages and talents, and that means you! Let your creative spirit free, choose any color you like, and make each beautiful image your own. There are no rules except to have fun.

Enjoy the process. Feel free to use colored pencils, pens, water colors, markers, and crayons—or any combination thereof—to add color and texture to each design. Notice that all the pictures are printed on just one side of the paper. To keep colors from bleeding through to the next page, simply slip an extra piece of paper underneath the page you're working on. When finished, you might like to remove the page from the book, trim it to size, and frame your artwork for all to see.

Most importantly, have fun with the process. Enjoy experimenting with contrasting colors or different shades of the same color. Try lighter hues for a softer look or layer and blend your colors for even more options. Allow some white space or saturate the entire piece with rich vibrant color, depending on your mood. Let your worries go, relax in the moment, and allow your creative spirit to lead the way!

Jehovah

LORD

THIS
IS MY NAME
FOREVER, THE NAME
YOU SHALL CALL ME FROM
GENERATION TO GENERATION.
EXODUS 3:15

THE LORD WHO PROVIDES

Jehovah-Jireh

And Abraham called
the name of the place,
The-LORD-Will-Provide.

GENESIS 22:14

El Shaddai
God Almighty

WHO IS LIKE YOU,
LORD GOD ALMIGHTY?
YOU, LORD, ARE MIGHTY, AND YOUR
FAITHFULNESS SURROUNDS YOU.
PSALM 89:8

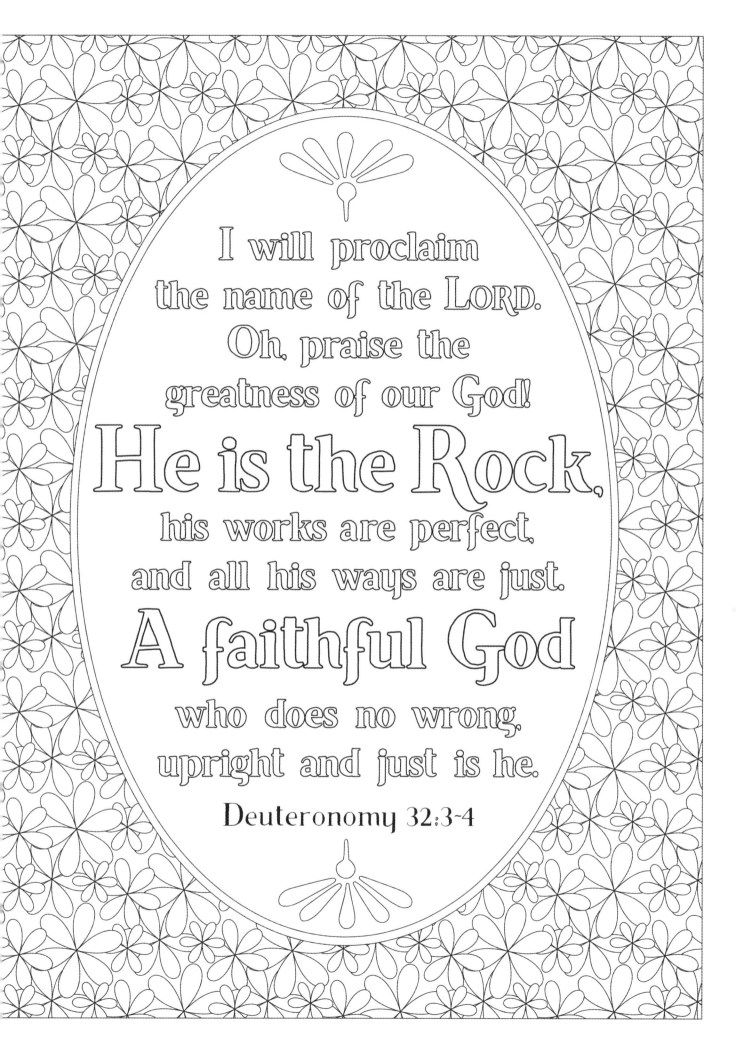

I will proclaim
the name of the LORD.
Oh, praise the
greatness of our God!
He is the Rock,
his works are perfect,
and all his ways are just.
A faithful God
who does no wrong,
upright and just is he.

Deuteronomy 32:3-4

Immanuel
GOD WITH US

The Lord himself will give you a sign: The virgin will conceive and give birth to a son, and will call him Immanuel. ISAIAH 7:14

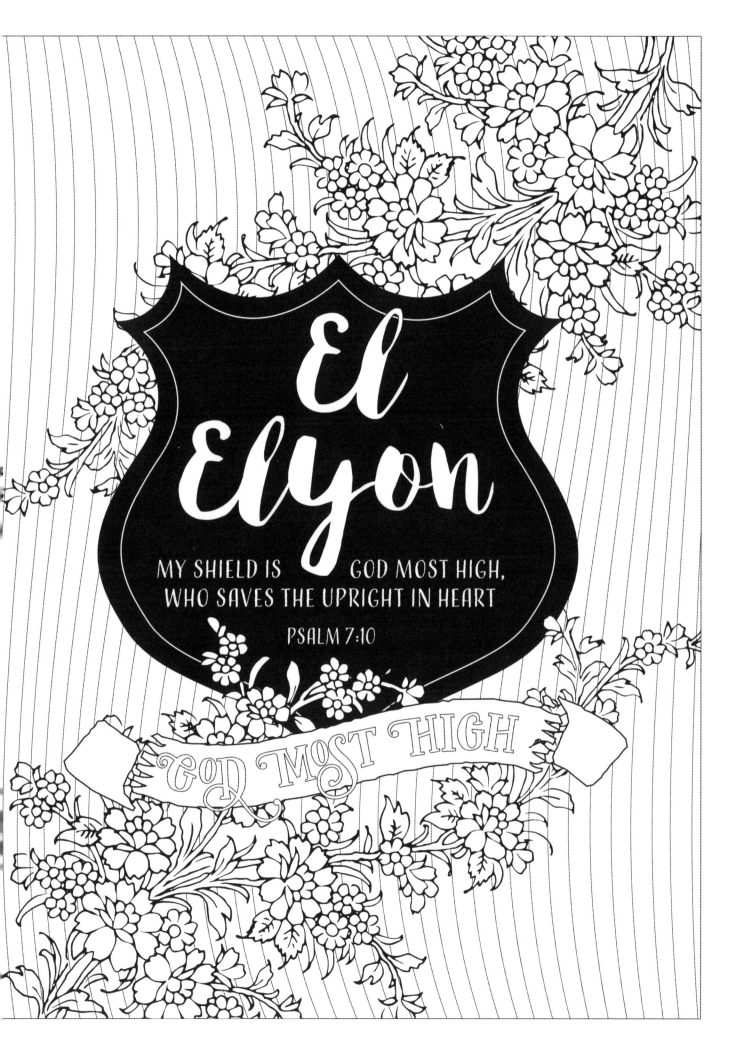

El Roi

The God Who Sees

You are the God who sees me.

Genesis 16:13

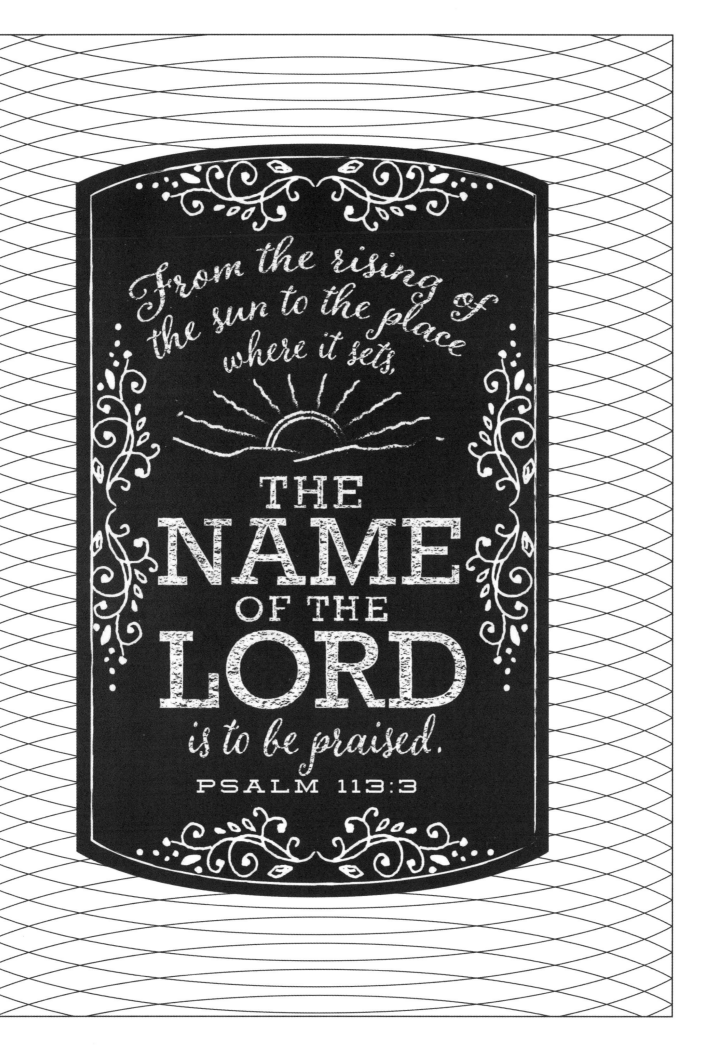

From the rising of the sun to the place where it sets,

THE NAME OF THE LORD is to be praised.

PSALM 113:3

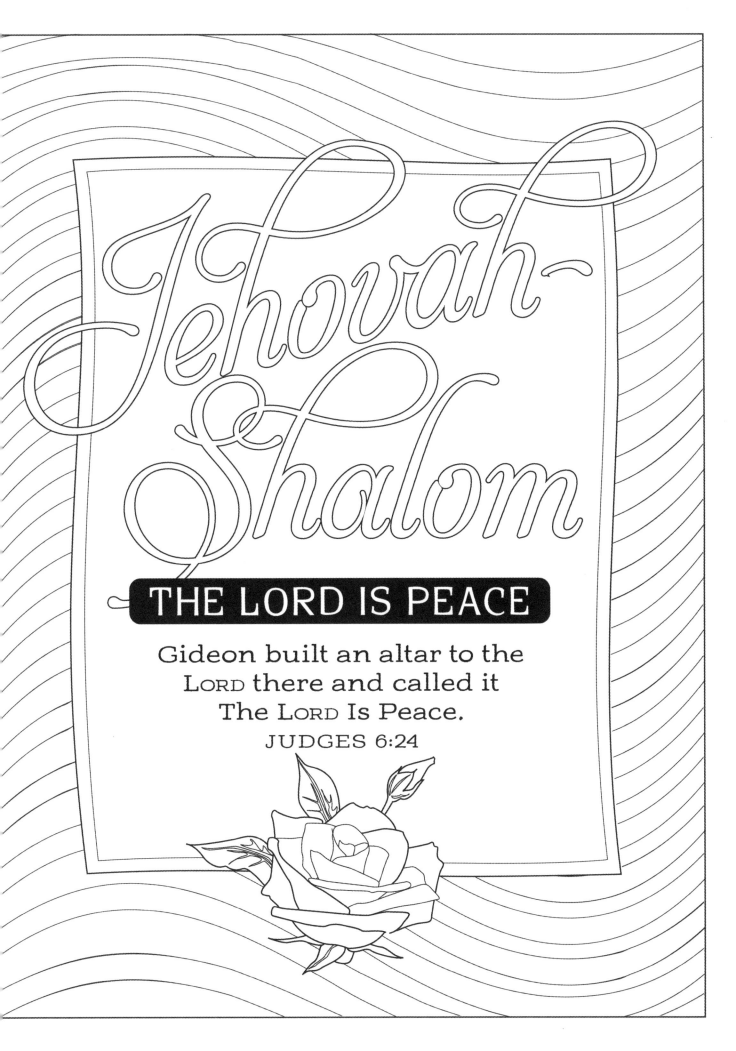

Jehovah-Shalom

THE LORD IS PEACE

Gideon built an altar to the
LORD there and called it
The LORD Is Peace.

JUDGES 6:24

El Olam

The Everlasting God

The LORD is the true God;
He is the living God
and the everlasting King.
Jeremiah 10:10

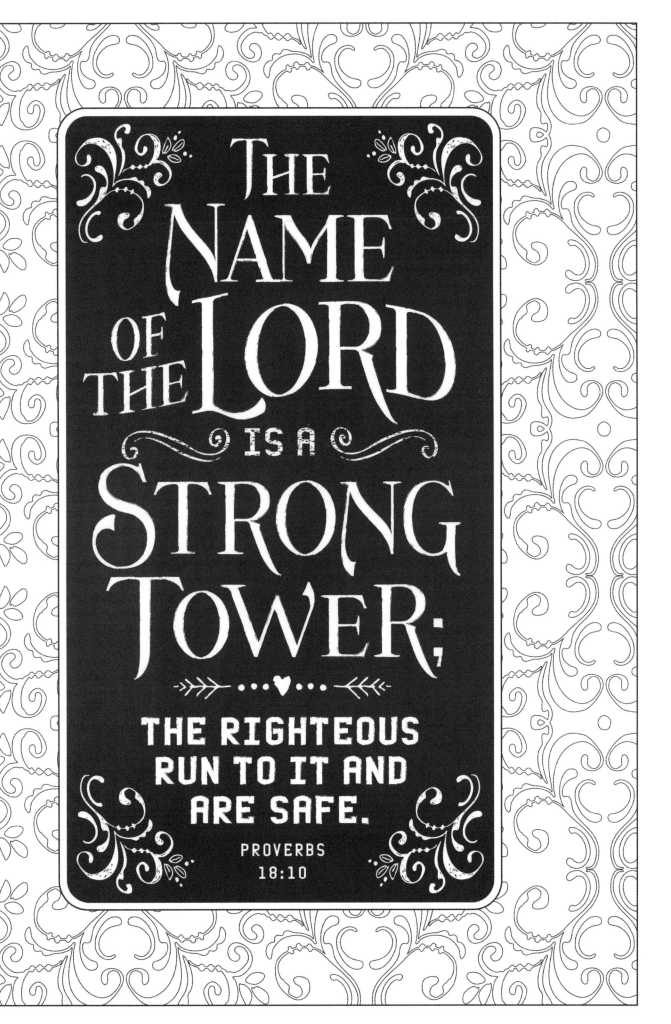

Jehovah-Rapha

THE LORD WHO HEALS

I am the LORD,
who heals you.
Exodus 15:26

Elohim

God

Be still, and know
that I am God.

Psalm 46:10

Jehovah-Sabaoth

THE LORD OF HOSTS

O Lord of hosts, How blessed is the man who trusts in You!

PSALM 84:12

JEHOVAH-
MEKODDISHKEM
The Lord Who Makes Holy

KEEP MY DECREES AND FOLLOW THEM.
I AM THE Lord, WHO MAKES YOU HOLY.
LEVITICUS 20:8

Adonai

LORD & MASTER

the fear of the
Lord—that is wisdom.

JOB 28:28

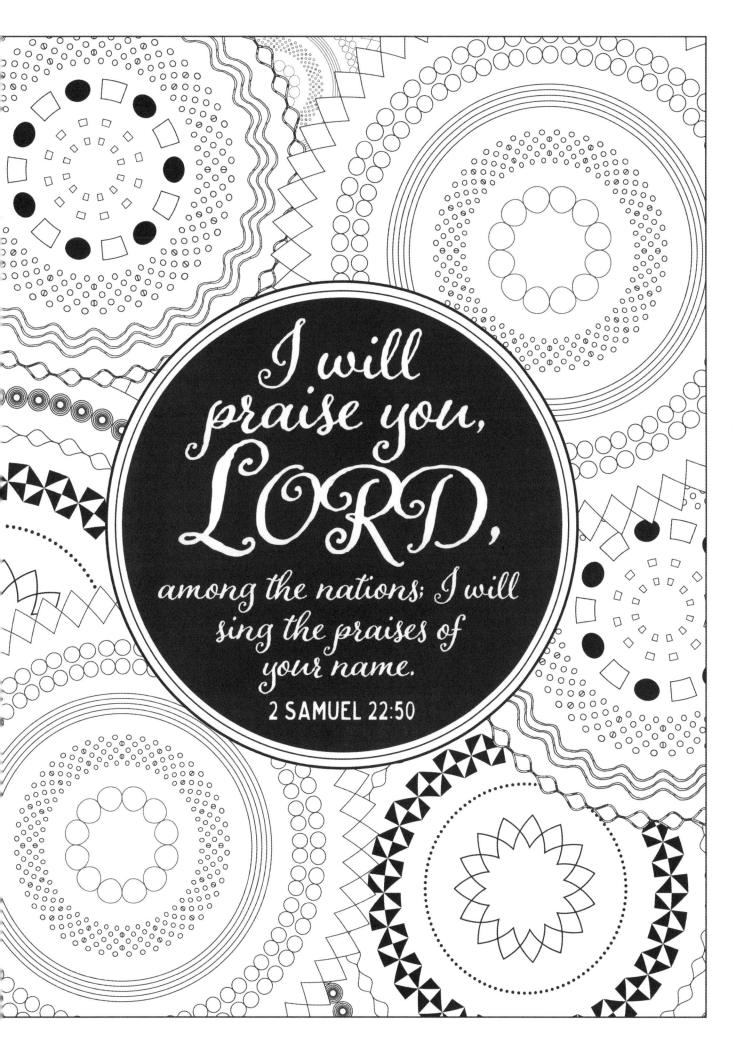

I will praise you, LORD, among the nations; I will sing the praises of your name.

2 SAMUEL 22:50

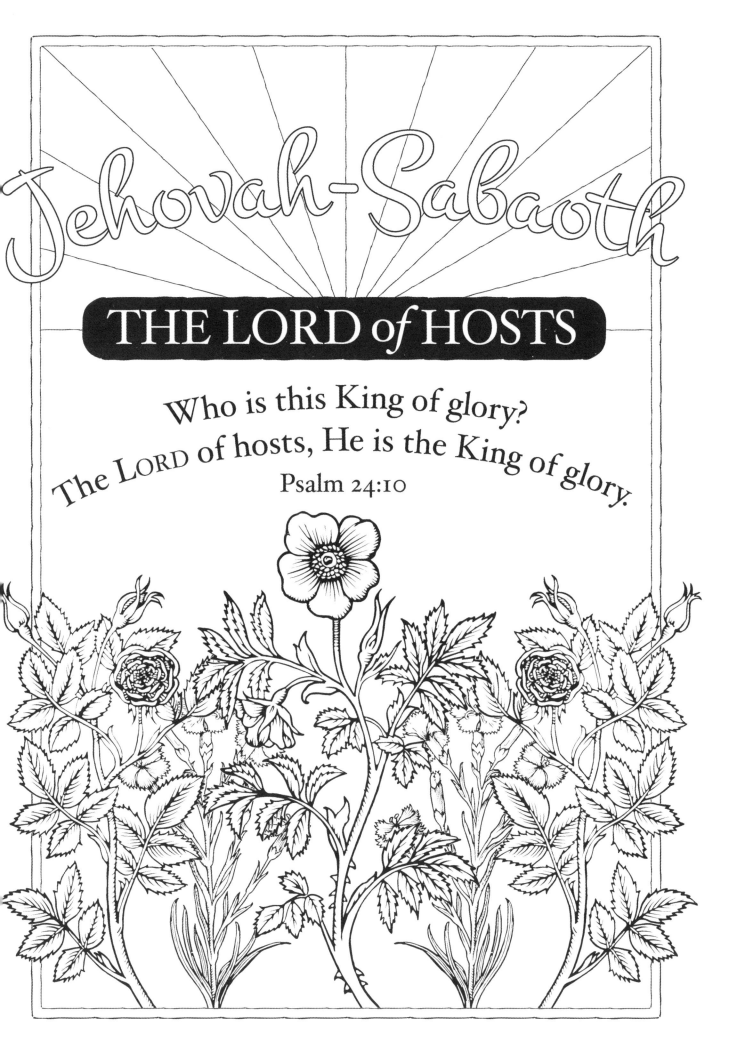

Jehovah-Sabaoth

THE LORD of HOSTS

Who is this King of glory?
The LORD of hosts, He is the King of glory.

Psalm 24:10

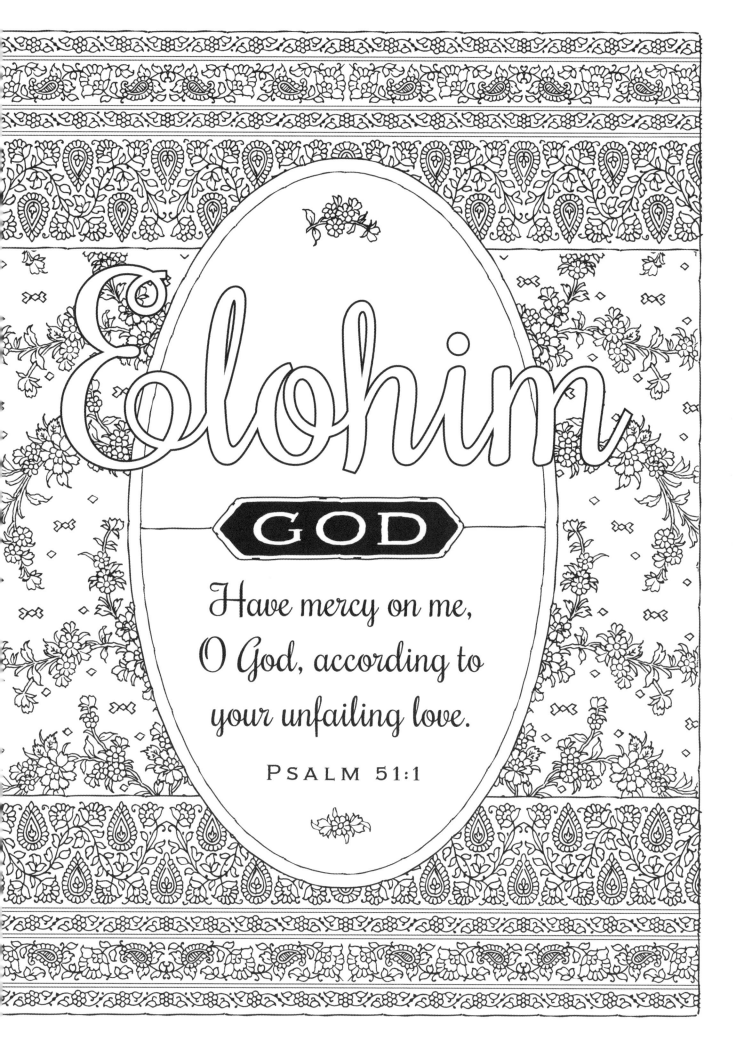

Elohim

GOD

Have mercy on me,
O God, according to
your unfailing love.

PSALM 51:1

Jehovah

LORD

From the LORD comes deliverance. May your blessing be on your people.

PSALM 3:8

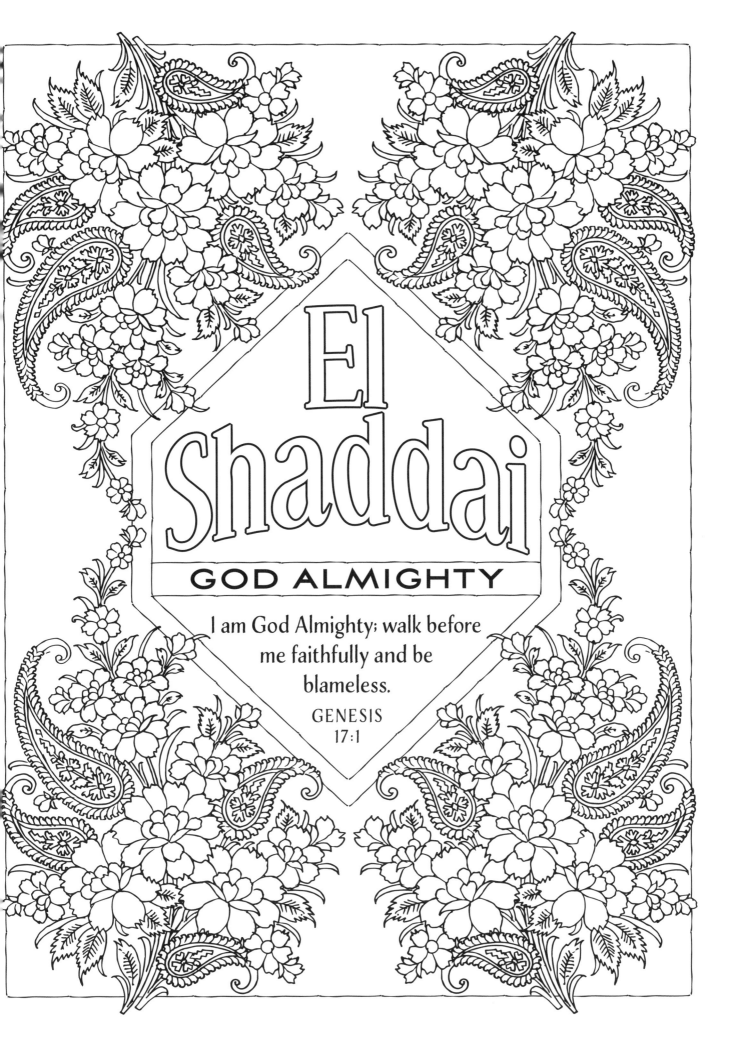

El Shaddai

GOD ALMIGHTY

I am God Almighty; walk before
me faithfully and be
blameless.

GENESIS
17:1

JEHOVAH-NISSI

The Lord My Banner

Moses built an altar
and called its name,
The~LORD~Is~My~Banner.

Exodus 17:15

Elohim
GOD

Truly my soul finds rest in God;
my salvation comes from him.

PSALM 62:1

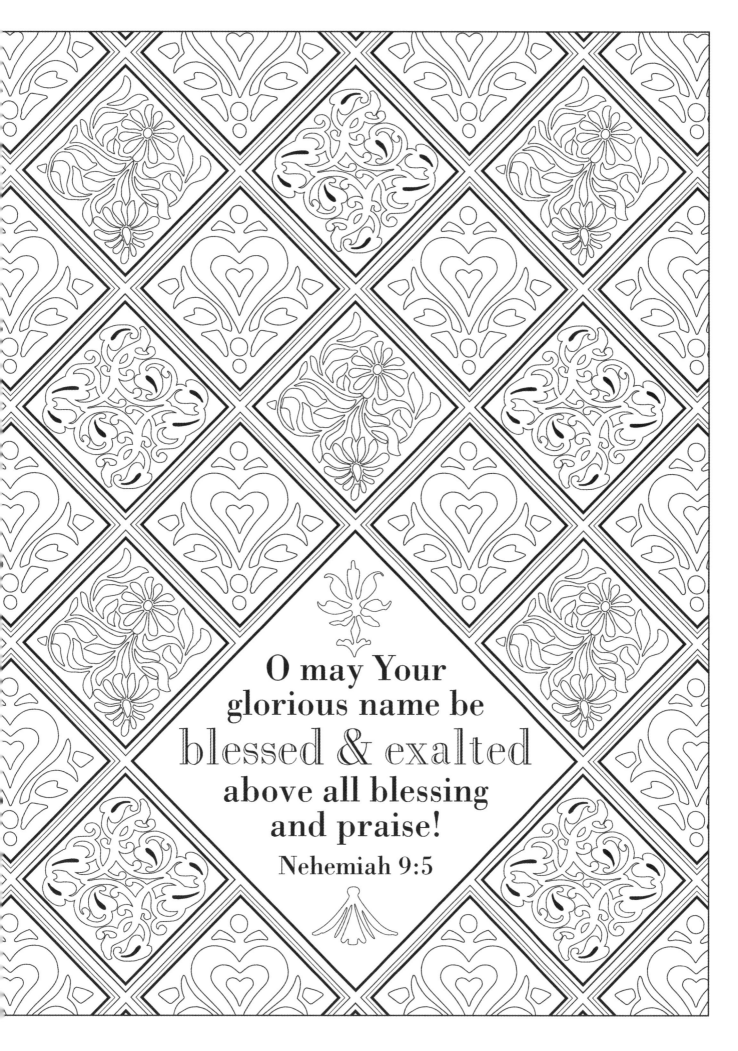

O may Your
glorious name be
blessed & exalted
above all blessing
and praise!

Nehemiah 9:5

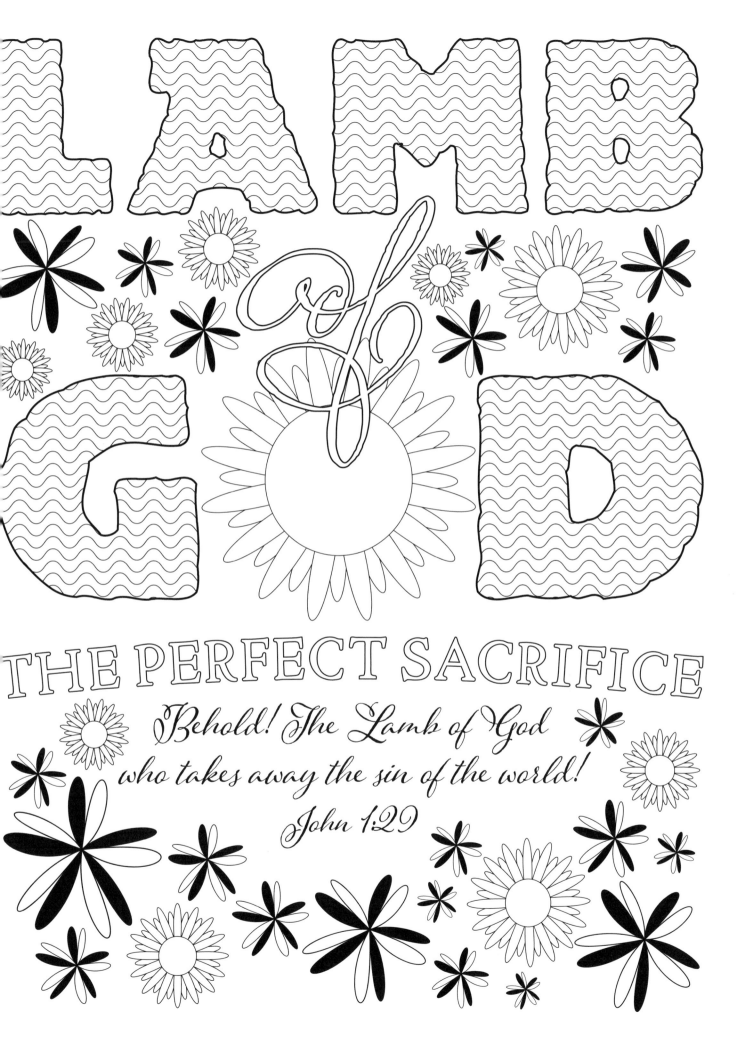

LAMB of GOD

THE PERFECT SACRIFICE

Behold! The Lamb of God
who takes away the sin of the world!

John 1:29

Those who went ahead and those who followed shouted,

Hosanna!

"Blessed is he who comes in the name of the Lord!"

Mark 11:9

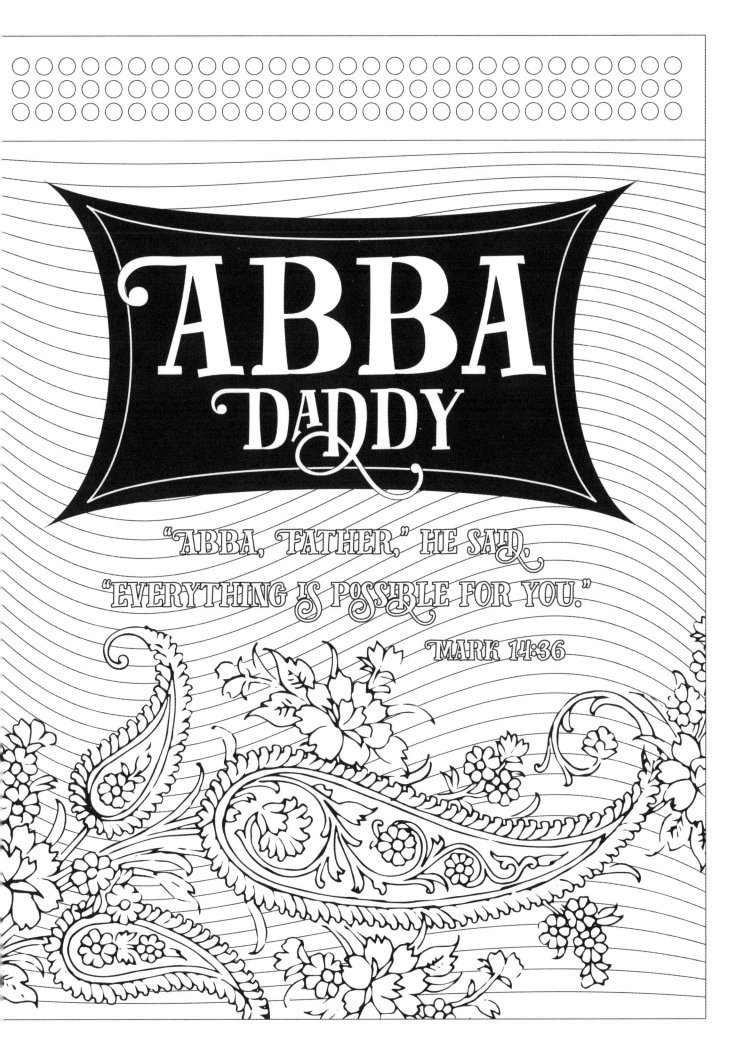

*A*ND EVERYONE WHO
CALLS ON THE NAME OF
THE LORD WILL BE SAVED.

ACTS 2:21

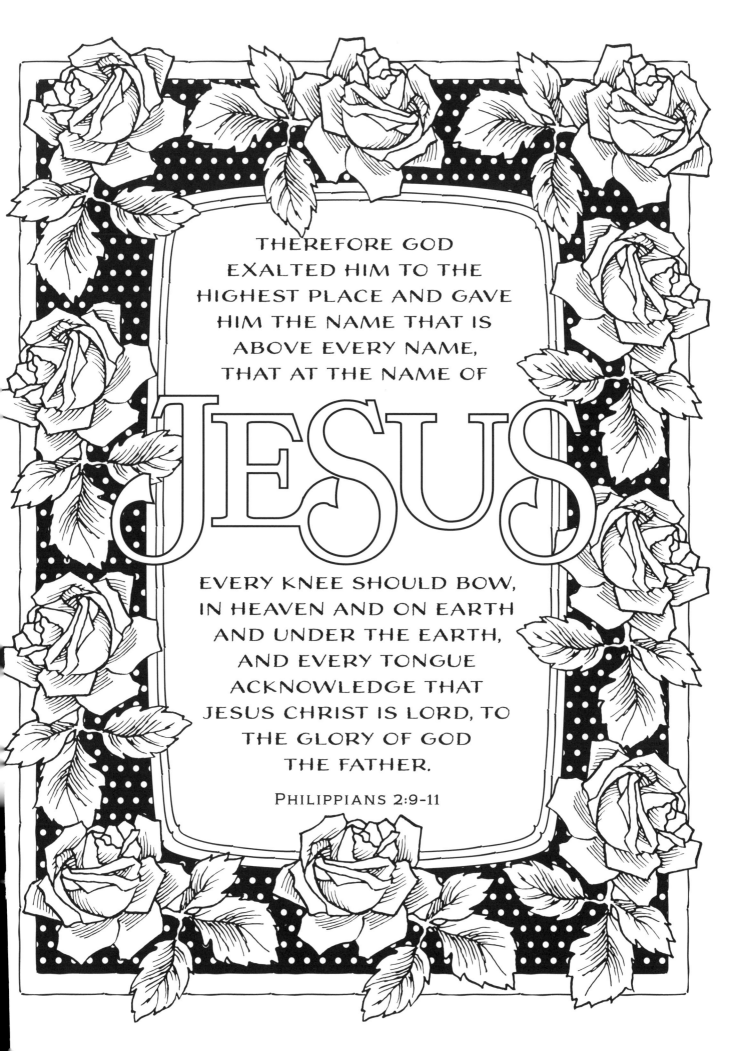

THEREFORE GOD EXALTED HIM TO THE HIGHEST PLACE AND GAVE HIM THE NAME THAT IS ABOVE EVERY NAME, THAT AT THE NAME OF

JESUS

EVERY KNEE SHOULD BOW, IN HEAVEN AND ON EARTH AND UNDER THE EARTH, AND EVERY TONGUE ACKNOWLEDGE THAT JESUS CHRIST IS LORD, TO THE GLORY OF GOD THE FATHER.

PHILIPPIANS 2:9-11

Marie Michaels represents the combined work of three artists from Dugan Design Group in Minneapolis, Minnesota: Nicole Wallace, Chris Dugan, and Terry Dugan. Their primary creative work is book cover and book interior design, increasingly focused on original content via illustration, photography, and digital media.

We'd love to see your creations!
Share your finished projects on social media with the hashtag

#colorthebible

We'll be looking for your artwork!

For information on more
Harvest House coloring books for adults, please visit
www.harvesthousepublishers.com